Writing
Quick Starts

Author: Linda Armstrong
Editor: Mary Dieterich
Proofreaders: Alexis Fey and Margaret Brown

COPYRIGHT © 2020 Mark Twain Media, Inc.

ISBN 978-1-62223-826-2

Printing No. CD-405058

Mark Twain Media, Inc., Publishers
Distributed by Carson-Dellosa Publishing LLC

The purchase of this book entitles the buyer to reproduce the student pages for classroom use only. Other permissions may be obtained by writing Mark Twain Media, Inc., Publishers.

All rights reserved. Printed in the United States of America.

Visit www.carsondellosa.com

Table of Contents

Introduction to the Teacher

To succeed in today's competitive environment, students must improve their writing skills. Quality classroom instruction remains the cornerstone of any writing program, but experienced teachers know that learning requires reinforcement. This book offers teachers and parents short quick start activities to help apprentice scribblers practice their craft. Used at the beginning of a language arts time slot, these mini-tasks help students focus on writing.

The pages are grouped into units covering such topics as Building Blocks, Everyday Writing, Nonfiction, Fiction, and Poetry.

Some activities offer inspiration. These include story prompts, suggestions for developing dynamic heroes and villains, poem starters, and challenges to create evocative scenes using all five senses.

Other activities review mechanical aspects of the writer's craft. These exercises guide students to use appropriate vocabulary, construct sentences, build paragraphs, and develop coherent fiction or nonfiction compositions.

Hint boxes are included with some activities to give students an idea of possible answers or words to include.

Reproduce the pages and cut along the lines, then use each section as a quick start to the day's lesson, or distribute copies of uncut pages for students to keep in a three-ring binder. Some activities, especially story leads and poem starters, will require additional sheets of paper for student responses.

The mini-activities make excellent transparencies. Share them with the class in any order.

Building Blocks of Great Writing

Building Blocks 1

Use each action verb in a sentence. Use your own paper if you need more space.

dashed _____

_____

grabbed _____

_____

attacked _____

_____

chased _____

_____

Building Blocks 2

Write each synonym next to its partner.

sofa   fowl

possess   buddy

friend _____

own _____

couch _____

bird _____

Building Blocks 3

Circle the form of "be" in each sentence.

He is an hour late.

She was the last one in line.

They were the first to arrive.

We are not alone.

Building Blocks 4

Draw lines to match the words that sound the same.

beech   pray

prey   waist

inn   beach

waste   in

Building Blocks of Great Writing

Building Blocks 5

Write the correct spelling beside each word.

shreek _____

repeet _____

recieve _____

(tree) lim _____

serprize _____

Building Blocks 6

Answer the question in a complete sentence.

Why should you use action verbs rather than forms of "be"?

_____

_____

_____

_____

_____

_____

Building Blocks 7

Write eight words for sounds.

_____

_____

_____

_____

_____

_____

_____

Building Blocks 8

Write eight words that describe your favorite food.

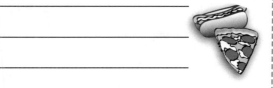

_____

_____

_____

_____

_____

_____

_____

Building Blocks of Great Writing

Building Blocks 9

Describe a place you hate without naming it.

_____

_____

_____

_____

_____

_____

_____

Building Blocks 10

Write eight words for colors.

_____

_____

_____

_____

_____

_____

_____

_____

Building Blocks 11

Describe a favorite movie star without naming him or her.

_____

_____

_____

_____

_____

_____

Building Blocks 12

Describe a cat. Use as many senses as possible.

_____

_____

_____

_____

_____

_____

_____

Building Blocks of Great Writing

Building Blocks 13

Close your eyes and picture a building. Describe it.

_____

_____

_____

_____

_____

_____

_____

_____

Building Blocks 14

Name eight sensations you experience through your skin.

_____

_____

_____

_____

_____

_____

_____

_____

Building Blocks 15

Describe an animal without naming it.

_____

_____

_____

_____

_____

_____

_____

Building Blocks 16

Name eight things you recognize by smell.

_____

_____

_____

_____

_____

_____

_____

_____

Building Blocks of Great Writing

Building Blocks 17

Write a description of the color orange for a person who is blind.

_____

_____

_____

_____

_____

_____

_____

Building Blocks 18

Describe an elephant. Use as many senses as possible.

_____

_____

_____

_____

_____

_____

_____

Building Blocks 19

If you lost your hearing today, what would you miss the most? Why?

_____

_____

_____

_____

_____

_____

_____

Building Blocks 20

Describe a fishing or cooking session. Use as many senses as possible.

_____

_____

_____

_____

_____

_____

_____

Building Blocks of Great Writing

Building Blocks 21

Circle the word that belongs in each sentence.

Everyone is going

(accept, except) us.

We are (all ready, already) to leave.

The (dessert, desert) is a place with

little water.

He is taller (than, then) she is.

Building Blocks 22

Draw a line to connect each misspelled word with the correct spelling.

neice	thought
sinserly	February
truely	sincerely
thout	niece
Febuary	truly

Building Blocks 23

Circle the correct spelling of the word in each line.

possability	posibility	possibility
receive	recieve	resceev
bulitin	bulletin	bulliten
thiefs	thieves	theives

Building Blocks 24

Circle the word that belongs in each sentence.

Tell Sam I will be (their, there).

I'll (see, sea) you later.

(You're, Your) my best friend.

Do you (no, know) how to do

long division?

(Who's, Whose) going to the

museum?

Building Blocks of Great Writing

Building Blocks 25

Write a sentence using each contraction.

it's _____

we're _____

you're _____

he's _____

I'm _____

Building Blocks 26

Add a subject to complete each sentence.

_____ raced down the street

toward home.

_____ kicked the ball over the fence.

_____ soared above town.

_____, my pet, does many tricks.

Building Blocks 27

Complete each sentence. Use an action verb in the predicate.

The old dog _____

_____

Jacob _____

_____

Our neighbor _____

_____

Building Blocks of Great Writing

Building Blocks 28

Circle the words that should be capitalized. Then rewrite the two sentences correctly on your own paper.

i looked for my desk. mr. peters said it was by the window.

we are going to the grand canyon for vacation. uncle james and aunt katie are going too.

Building Blocks 29

Put a caret (^) where each period belongs. Then rewrite the two sentences correctly on your own paper.

Mrs Hernandez reads to us every day after lunch I missed the chapter yesterday because I had to see Dr Lee

I sat next to Paulo at lunch Stephen and Jamal sat with us too

Building Blocks 30

Circle the sentence that does not belong in the paragraph.

My brother had a party last week. His birthday was the first day of summer vacation, and it was almost ninety degrees outside. I like chocolate better than vanilla. We met his friends at Wacky Waves Water Park for a day of slipping and splashing. I even went off the diving board! It was the best celebration ever!

Everyday Writing

Everyday Writing 1

What belongs in the top right-hand corner of a friendly letter?

_____

What belongs at the end of a friendly letter?

_____

In a friendly letter, do you indent the paragraphs, or skip a line between them?

_____

Hint Box: closing, greeting, body heading

Everyday Writing 2

These are possible closings for friendly letters. Circle the ones that are incorrect.

Yours Truely:

yours truly,

Your friend,

Sincerely,

Sincerly Yours,

Until then,

Everyday Writing 3

This is the return address section of a friendly letter. Circle the errors. Write the address correctly.

Three hundred two frog ave

lupineville ca 55555

apr 24 2020

_____

_____

_____

Everyday Writing 4

On your own paper, write a letter inviting a friend to a party.

Hint Box: R.S.V.P., birthday, holiday, celebration, barbecue

Everyday Writing

Everyday Writing 5

Name each section of a friendly letter.

a. _____

b. _____

c. _____

    _____

    _____

May 2

Dear Mary,
Please come to my
house on May 8 at
noon. We can take
my dog, Rags, to
the school pet show.
We'll have fun!

Your friend,
Jenny

d. _____

Everyday Writing 6

On the lines below, write a short letter thanking your grandfather for a present.

_____

_____

_____

_____

_____

_____

Everyday Writing 7

Name the parts of a business letter.

a. _____

b. _____

c. _____

d. _____

    _____

e. _____

Hint Box:

address

inside

return

closing

body

greeting

Everyday Writing

Everyday Writing 8

On your own paper, write a letter to a friend who is spending the summer in another state.

Hint Box: already, forget, funny, wondering, neighbor, vacation

Everyday Writing 9

On your own paper, write a letter to relatives you seldom see. Tell them about something funny that happened at home.

Hint Box: broke, dropped, forgot, locked, joke, lost, believed

Everyday Writing 10

On your own paper, write a letter to your neighbors thanking them for saving cans for your school's recycling program.

Hint Box: recycling, important, helpful, civic, protect, purchase

Everyday Writing 11

Imagine you are away at summer camp. On your own paper, write a letter to your parents or your friends back home.

Hint Box: cabin, counselor, campfire, hiking, mosquitoes, horses, flashlight, restroom

Everyday Writing

Everyday Writing 12

Write the inside address for a business letter to Mr. William Arden at Middleville News. His office is at 7650 Median St. in Arizona (AZ). The zip code is 50000. The name of the town is Middleville.

_____

_____

_____

_____

_____

Everyday Writing 13

On your own paper, write a business letter to Mr. Carson Trainz asking for a job at Hobby Hill. The address of the shop is 224 Third Street, Big Hill, ME 78122.

Everyday Writing 14

On your own paper, write a business letter to Mrs. Al Waygood-Newz, editor of the _Nicetown Gazette._ Tell her about an interesting class project. The address of her office is 66915 S. Industrial Ave., Nicetown, CO 81010.

Everyday Writing 15

On your own paper, write a business letter to Miss Kinda Lisning, head of the complaint department at Junky Electronics, Incorporated. Tell her that your new micropter camcorder watch broke when you opened the box. You are returning it, and you want a new one. The company is located at 123456 S. Runaround Blvd., Tradestown, NJ 45678.

Everyday Writing

Everyday Writing 16

Write a phone message for your mom. Tell her Joe Tuneup called about her car. Invent Joe's message and the phone number. Complete sentences are not necessary.

_____

_____

_____

_____

_____

_____

_____

Everyday Writing 17

Your teacher just assigned a history report. Circle the four phrases you would write in your assignment book.

must be good

due on April 24

3–5 pages long

use ink or word processor

teacher likes ice cream

Subject: Education in the Colonies

Everyday Writing 18

Circle the most informative phrases. Use them to create a flyer on your own paper.

Friday, Oct. 5 at 7 p.m.
or   Friday Night

Don't Miss It!
or   Talent Show!

Eastgate School Auditorium
or   Eastgate

$2 per person
or   Not Free

Everyday Writing 19

On your own paper, write directions from your classroom to the main office. Include landmarks such as stairs, display cases, double doors, and restrooms.

Everyday Writing

Everyday Writing 20

Write directions for making a phone call.

1. _____
_____

2. _____
_____

3. _____
_____

4. _____
_____

Everyday Writing 21

Write an e-mail message to your friend asking for information about a homework assignment.

Subject: _____

Greeting: _____

Message: _____

_____

_____

_____

Closing: _____

Everyday Writing 22

Write a journal entry about what has happened since you arrived at school today.

_____

_____

_____

_____

_____

_____

_____

Everyday Writing 23

Write a journal entry about something in the news this week.

_____

_____

_____

_____

_____

_____

_____

Everyday Writing

Everyday Writing 24

Write a journal entry about the best thing that happened this month.

_____

_____

_____

_____

_____

_____

_____

Everyday Writing 25

Write a journal entry about what you are studying in science, geography, or history.

_____

_____

_____

_____

_____

_____

_____

Everyday Writing 26

Write a journal entry about something you can't forget.

_____

_____

_____

_____

_____

_____

Everyday Writing 27

Write a journal entry about something to which you are looking forward.

_____

_____

_____

_____

_____

_____

_____

Everyday Writing

Everyday Writing 28

Write a journal entry about something you dread.

_____

_____

_____

_____

_____

_____

_____

Everyday Writing 29

Write a journal entry about something you expect to happen later today or tonight.

_____

_____

_____

_____

_____

_____

_____

Everyday Writing 30

Write a journal entry about your last vacation, holiday, or school break.

_____

_____

_____

_____

_____

_____

Everyday Writing 31

Circle six words to use in the review of a <u>good</u> action movie.

boring	sentimental
exciting	star
disappointed	chase
suspense	fought
battle	crying

Everyday Writing

Everyday Writing 32

Pick a movie you know well. Describe what it is about.

_____

_____

_____

_____

_____

_____

_____

_____

Everyday Writing 33

Name a movie or TV series you don't like. Tell why you don't like it.

_____

_____

_____

_____

_____

_____

_____

Everyday Writing 34

Write an opinion poll question for students at your school.

Question: _____

_____

_____

Choices:

a. _____

b. _____

c. _____

Everyday Writing 35

Recommend a book to a friend (without giving away any spoilers).

You should read _____

_____

The best part is _____

_____

_____

_____

_____

Everyday Writing

Everyday Writing 36

The Civil War, sometimes called the War Between the States, was long and bloody. Name three causes of the Civil War.

Circle the phrase below that tells what the completed answer must include.

dates of major battles

three reasons the war began

the names of leaders

Everyday Writing 37

Most plants need light, water, air, and soil. Explain why plants need light.

Circle the phrase below that tells what the explanation to the statement above should include.

things plants need

how plants use water

how plants use light

Everyday Writing 38

Here is an answer: *The tubes that carry blood throughout the body are called arteries, veins, and capillaries. Arteries carry blood from the heart to the rest of the body. Veins carry blood back to the heart. Capillaries deliver the blood to the cells.*

Write the question. _____

_____

_____

Everyday Writing

Everyday Writing 39

Answer this essay question:

What causes day and night? _____

_____

_____

_____

_____

Hint Box:
axis
twenty-four
rotates
Earth
sun
hours

Everyday Writing 40

Why are writing skills important? _____

_____

_____

_____

_____

_____

Everyday Writing 41

Why are good health habits important? _____

_____

_____

_____

_____

_____

Everyday Writing

Everyday Writing 42

Circle every error in this paragraph. Rewrite it correctly on your own paper.

Their are thowsandz of kinds of insecs insecs have six legs there bodys are divided into tree parts an insec has a head a thorax and an abdomen an aunt is an insec but a spider isn't.

Everyday Writing 43

Circle every error in this paragraph. Rewrite it correctly on your own paper.

waetr takes many formz waetr evaporates form the surface of the see it turns into clowds. some of the waetr in clowds falls down as rayn and snow. The raynwaetr runs downhill into rivers and streams until it reachs the see. Waetrs journey is called the water cicle.

Everyday Writing 44

What is the most important writing rule? Why?

_____

_____

_____

_____

_____

_____

_____

Everyday Writing 45

Why is honesty important?

_____

_____

_____

_____

_____

_____

_____

_____

Nonfiction

Nonfiction 1

Add a place name and supporting sentences to complete the paragraph.

If you have never visited

_____, you

should go because _____

_____

_____

_____

_____

Nonfiction 2

Add a place name below. Then, on your own paper, write supporting sentences to complete the paragraph.

If I could fly anywhere in the world,

I would buy a ticket for

_____.

Nonfiction 3

Tell about your first memory.

_____

_____

_____

_____

_____

_____

_____

Nonfiction 4

Tell about your first day of kindergarten or first grade.

_____

_____

_____

_____

_____

_____

_____

Nonfiction

Nonfiction 5

Name a restaurant. Then tell what the place looks like and what you like to order.

On special occasions, I like to eat at _____.

The setting _____

_____

The food _____

_____

Nonfiction 6

If you could have any job when you are thirty years old, what would it be?

_____

_____

_____

_____

_____

Nonfiction 7

Where would you like to live when you are twenty-five?

_____

_____

_____

_____

_____

Nonfiction

Nonfiction 8

Write about a family event you attended.

_____

_____

_____

_____

_____

Nonfiction 9

Which is better, being an only child or having brothers and/or sisters? Why?

_____

_____

_____

_____

_____

Nonfiction 10

What do you like about the street or area where you live? What don't you like?

_____

_____

_____

_____

Nonfiction

Nonfiction 11

List three keywords you might use when searching for information about the Revolutionary War in the library or on the Internet.

_____

_____

_____

Nonfiction 12

Which reference work below presents general information about many subjects?

_____

Hint Box:

thesaurus

encyclopedia

atlas

dictionary

Nonfiction 13

Circle the best topic for a two-page research report. Explain your choice.

fur on bears' ears   sea creatures

camels   land mammals

snake eyelids

_____

_____

_____

_____

Nonfiction 14

You are doing a report on vegetables, and you find a great book about farming. List three words to look up in the index.

_____

_____

_____

_____

Nonfiction

Nonfiction 15

Circle the best topic for a two-page research report. Explain your choice.

Causes of the Civil War

The Civil War

The History of the United States

Abraham Lincoln's Hat

_____

_____

_____

_____

_____

Nonfiction 16

When researching a report about snails, which source would you use first? Why?

_____

_____

_____

_____

_____

_____

Nonfiction 17

Circle items to include when taking notes from a reference book.

information

author

librarian's age

page number

book title

publication date

library card number

date due

Nonfiction 18

Check the correct answer.

When is it acceptable to copy part of a book into your report?

_____ It is never acceptable.

_____ It is acceptable to quote a sentence if you use quotation marks and give the source.

_____ It is acceptable to copy as much as you need.

Nonfiction

Nonfiction 19

Circle the three primary sources.

an encyclopedia

a personal interview

a biography

an almanac

a book of lists

a pioneer diary

a soldier's letter

a Wikipedia article

Nonfiction 20

Why is it a good idea to use several sources when you are doing research for a report?

_____

_____

_____

_____

Nonfiction 21

Underline the words you would copy if you were taking notes from this paragraph.

   In our solar system, eight planets orbit a star we call the sun. Mercury is the closest to the sun. Next come Venus, Earth, and Mars. The largest planet, Jupiter, is closer than Saturn and Uranus. Neptune is the farthest away.

Nonfiction

Nonfiction 22

Add the words in the box to the outline in the correct places below.

I. _____

   A. _____

   B. _____

      1. _____

      2. _____

Word Bank: Mercury, Earth, Solar System, Planets, Sun

Nonfiction 23

Use this outline to write a paragraph on your own paper.

I. Pets

   A. Dogs

   B. Cats

   C. Tropical Fish

Nonfiction 24

Make an outline for a paragraph about snacks you like.

I. _____

   A. _____

   B. _____

   C. _____

Nonfiction 25

On your own paper, make an outline for an essay about how to play your favorite game.

Nonfiction

Nonfiction 26

Circle the sentence that is out of order. Rewrite the paragraph on your own paper.

January hosted the Wolf Moon. May basked under the Flower Moon. Native Americans gave a name to each full moon. The Buck Moon graced July, and the Hunter's Moon illuminated October.

Nonfiction 27

Fill in the blanks with the correct word for each sentence.

though   **thorough**   **through**

When a tornado whirls _____ a town, it destroys many buildings.

He did a _____ job of cleaning the workstation.

He knew the answer, _____ he didn't speak.

Nonfiction 28

Fill in the blanks with the correct word for each sentence.

laid   **lay**   **lie**

Ancient streams _____ down pebbles and mud that turned into a kind of rock called conglomerate.

She was sick and had to _____ down.

I'll _____ the book on the table.

Nonfiction

Nonfiction 29

Fill in the blanks with the correct word for each sentence.

laid   **lay**   **lie**

General Grant wanted to _____ down and rest.

Abraham Lincoln _____ the book aside and rested.

They told him to _____ the map on the desk.

Nonfiction 30

Rewrite the following sentence. Add the missing commas.

The parts of the ear are the outer ear the eardrum the cochlea and the auditory nerve.

_____

_____

_____

Nonfiction 31

Rewrite the following sentences. Add the missing punctuation.

William Shakespeare died on April 23 1616 He was fifty-two years old

_____

_____

_____

_____

Nonfiction

Nonfiction 32

Fill in the blanks with the correct word for each sentence.

breathe   **breath**

He was out of _____.

He couldn't _____.

except   **accept**

I got everything _____ the milk.

Will you _____ the award?

Nonfiction 33

Circle the extra words. Rewrite the sentence correctly.

The very important legislative branch of our country's government constantly makes our country's legal laws.

_____

_____

_____

_____

_____

Nonfiction 34

Join these two sentences with the word "but." Write the new sentence below.

There were fifty-five delegates to the Constitutional Convention. Many were absent.

_____

_____

_____

_____

Nonfiction 35

Circle the misspelled words. Rewrite the sentence correctly.

In 1849 thosands of gold minors bot suplys and rushed too California.

_____

_____

_____

_____

Nonfiction

Nonfiction 36

Join these two sentences with the word "because." Write the new sentence below.

Dolley Madison had to leave the White House. The British burned it down.

_____

 _____

_____

Nonfiction 37

Use the word "when" to make these two sentences into one. Write the new sentence below.

Immigrant Mormons couldn't afford covered wagons.

They used handcarts.

_____

_____

_____

Nonfiction 38

Combine these three sentences into one. Write the new sentence below.

George Washington was President of the United States. John Adams was President of the United States. James Monroe was President of the United States.

_____

_____

_____

Nonfiction

Nonfiction 39

Fill in the word that belongs in each sentence.

circle   **circles**

A flock of gulls _____ above the Great Salt Lake.

is   **are**

The pioneer family _____ determined to reach Oregon.

drive   **drives**

A teamster _____ a team of mules with supplies for the miners.

was   **were**

The Forty-Niners _____ willing to risk it all to strike it rich.

Nonfiction 40

Write the correct word in each sentence.

begin   **began**

Paul Revere jumped on the horse and _____ to ride.

The cabin boy couldn't wait for the voyage to _____.

creeps   **crept**

The scout _____ over the hill and checked on the enemy camp.

As the sunlight _____ through the windows, I do my best to wake up.

take   **took**

How long did it _____ to get from Independence to Sacramento?

Most wagon trains _____ a route through the mountains.

Fiction

Fiction 1

Name four hopes or dreams a character might have.

Someday I'll _____

_____

Someday I'll _____

_____

Someday _____

_____

Someday _____

_____

Fiction 2

Describe the oldest man in the world.

_____

_____

_____

_____

_____

_____

_____

_____

Fiction 3

Describe a mother.

_____

_____

_____

_____

_____

_____

_____

_____

Fiction

Fiction 4

Characters in stories have jobs to do. Name as many jobs as you can in the space below.

_____

_____

_____

_____

_____

_____

Fiction 5

Describe someone who is very good at his/her job. Tell why he/she is good at it and how he/she feels about doing a good job.

_____

_____

_____

_____

_____

_____

_____

Fiction 6

A conflict is the main problem that characters face in a story. List four things people argue about.

_____

_____

_____

_____

_____

_____

_____

Fiction 7

Name two things that make people envious.

_____

_____

_____

_____

_____

_____

_____

Fiction

Fiction 8

Name two reasons best friends fight.

_____

_____

_____

_____

_____

_____

_____

_____

Fiction 9

A conflict can be within the main character or with other characters or outside forces. List three problems boys or girls have at school.

_____

_____

_____

_____

_____

_____

_____

_____

Fiction 10

List three problems boys or girls have at home.

_____

_____

_____

_____

_____

_____

_____

_____

Fiction 11

You live with your father in a secret lab under the North Pole. On your own paper, write a paragraph about eating breakfast.

Fiction

Fiction 12

It is the year 1875. On your own paper, write a paragraph about your trip home from school.

Fiction 13

An alien monster is in your house. On your own paper, write a paragraph to convince your parents the monster is real.

Fiction 14

Your plane has crashed on a mountain in Colorado. It is the middle of winter. On your own paper, write a paragraph about waking up at the crash site and what you do next.

Fiction 15

It is the year 2531. On your own paper, write a paragraph about your trip to school.

Fiction

Fiction 16

Write a paragraph about a dog who wants to trade places with its owner.

_____

_____

_____

_____

_____

_____

_____

Fiction 17

Write a paragraph about an action hero who is afraid.

_____

_____

_____

_____

_____

_____

_____

_____

Fiction 18

Write a paragraph about a lost brother or sister.

_____

_____

_____

_____

_____

_____

_____

_____

Fiction 19

On your own paper, write a paragraph about a boy whose curiosity gets him into trouble.

Fiction

Fiction 20

List six feelings. Your main character has a problem because of one of these feelings. Write the story on your own paper.

_____

_____

_____

_____

_____

Fiction 21

On your own paper, write the story of "The Three Bears" from the point of view of Baby Bear's friend, Little Squirrel, who lives in a neighboring tree. Make some notes here.

_____

_____

_____

_____

_____

_____

Fiction 22

Choose a book, movie, or TV show. In one sentence, name the main character and his or her problem in the story.

_____

_____

_____

_____

_____

_____

Fiction 23

Think of the bad guy, or villain, in any book, movie, or TV show. In one sentence, tell what the villain wants in the story.

_____

_____

_____

_____

_____

_____

Fiction

Fiction 24

Choose any book, movie, or TV show. In one sentence, name the main character and tell what he or she wants. For example, Cinderella wants to escape from her stepmother and stepsisters.

_____

_____

_____

_____

_____

_____

Fiction 25

Pretend that there is a dolphin that helps people in trouble. On your own paper, tell about one of the dolphin's rescues.

Fiction 26

Stories often pit heroes against nature. List at least four kinds of natural disasters.

_____

_____

_____

_____

_____

_____

_____

Fiction 27

Invent a heroine. In one sentence, tell how she helps someone survive a natural disaster.

_____

_____

_____

_____

_____

_____

_____

_____

Fiction

Fiction 28

Invent a hero. Write a few lines of dialogue between the hero and the villain. Don't forget to use correct punctuation.

_____

_____

_____

_____

_____

_____

_____

_____

Fiction 29

Who is the villain in "Snow White and the Seven Dwarfs"?

_____

_____

On your own paper, tell the story from the villain's point of view.

Fiction 30

Many story heroes have a helper or sidekick. List three ways friends can help each other.

_____

_____

_____

_____

_____

_____

_____

_____

Fiction

Fiction 31

On your own paper, write a story about a girl who defeats a monster with the help of a pet.

Fiction 32

On your own paper, write a story about a boy who finds a magic eraser. Where does he find it? How does it help him? How does it get him into trouble?

Fiction 33

Characters in stories are often the biggest, the best, or the worst. For example, Hercules was the strongest man in the world. On your

own paper, list four examples of extreme qualities characters might possess.

Fiction 34

Unscramble five examples of good traits heroes or heroines might possess.

racugeo _____

nesnkids _____

yaltyol _____

tyeshon _____

tyerogsien _____

Fiction

Fiction 35

Find and circle four bad characteristics of a villain that are hidden in the puzzle to the right.

Write them on the lines below.

1. _____
2. _____
3. _____
4. _____

T	Y	Z	A	L
A	V	L	L	E
E	N	I	T	K
H	E	A	R	B
C	H	R	T	N

Fiction 36

Courage is often the subject of stories and books. Write a paragraph about a situation where courage would be important.

_____

_____

_____

_____

_____

_____

_____

_____

_____

Fiction

Fiction 37

Greed is often the subject of books and stories. List six things people want so much that they will do anything to get them.

_____

_____

_____

_____

_____

Fiction 38

In some stories, a hero overcomes fear. List six things people fear.

_____

_____

_____

_____

_____

_____

Fiction 39

Power is often the subject of stories and books. Give an example of a person who has (or had) too much power. What did they do with their power?

_____

_____

_____

_____

_____

Fiction 40

Love is often the subject of stories and books. Name a person, animal, place, and thing you love.

_____

_____

_____

_____

Poetry

Poetry 1

Write a cinquain on your own paper. Use this form.

noun

adjective, adjective

-ing word, -ing word, -ing word

prepositional phrase

noun

Poetry 2

Circle two subjects for a summer haiku, and then add two of your own.

frozen lake   sunflowers

sand   snowflakes

_____   _____

Poetry 3

Name a person, place, and two things. Use them to write an unrhymed poem on your own paper.

person: _____

place: _____

thing: _____

thing: _____

Poetry 4

Close your eyes. Write five lines about the first thing that pops into your mind.

_____

_____

_____

_____

_____

Poetry

Poetry 5

Write a winter haiku. Copy the poem to your own paper and create an illustration to go along with it.

_____ 5 syllables

_____ 7 syllables

_____ 5 syllables

Poetry 6

Write a four-line poem using a color, a texture, and onomatopoeia.

_____

_____

_____

_____

Poetry 7

Finish this limerick.

There was a young lady named S_____

   (rhymes with _moo_)

Who once thought that zebras said, "Moo."

She painted a c_____ (rhymes with _how_)

and started a row (rhymes with _how_ and means a _ruckus_)

When she took the poor beast to the _____ (rhymes with _moo_).

Write your own limerick on another sheet of paper.

Poetry

Poetry 8

Onomatopoeia means using words to create sound effects. On your own paper, use each sound-effect word in a sentence.

roared   barked

hissed   chirped

Poetry 9

Unscramble these texture words.

yolwo: _____

loysgs: _____

lkics: _____

ugroh: _____

eratyleh: _____

Poetry 10

Circle the sound words. (Words may continue in next line.)

ranquackname
oinkstreetwoo
fmeowsqueak
honkfloorhum
neightable

Poetry 11

Draw a line to connect two words that name a similar color.

emerald   red

scarlet   purple

amber   green

sapphire   yellow

amethyst   blue

Poetry

Poetry 12

Write six words that rhyme with *cold.*

_____

_____

_____

_____

_____

_____

Poetry 13

Finish this hink pink.

What do you call a case of the sniffles that lasts for years?

An _____ cold

Write a hink pink and a clue of your own.

Clue: _____

_____

_____

Answer: _____

Poetry 14

Lewis Carroll wrote a funny version of "Twinkle, Twinkle, Little Star" called "Twinkle, Twinkle, Little Bat." On your own paper, write your own version of a familiar song.

Poetry 15

Write a silly two-line poem, or couplet. End each line with a word that rhymes with *toe.*

_____

_____

_____

_____

_____

_____

Poetry

Poetry 16

Circle the words that have more than one meaning in this poem.

"Shoo, shoo, fly!" I say. "Fly, fly away!"

Not a fly fan, I fan, and I fan,

Then dump out my pencils and wait

till he lands.

Now can I capture him under the can?

Poetry 17

Poets often use words with more than one meaning. Circle all of the meanings of *still*.

talk

quiet

to stop noise

without waves

unmoving

a photograph

continuing

friend

Poetry 18

Unscramble the word that solves the analogy.

Clock is to *time* as _____

is to *temperature*. (mtteeremohr)

Dog is to *pet* as *spoon* is to

_____. (rlvwsreiea)

Poetry 19

Analogies are comparisons. Solve these analogies.

Night is to *day* as *dark* is to

_____.

Blouse is to *girl* as *shirt* is to

_____.

Love is to *hate* as *tall* is to

_____.

Morning is to _____

as *evening* is to *night*.

Poetry

Poetry 20

Circle the word that solves the analogy.

Flock is to *bird* as

_____ is to *lion*.

yellowmaneprideschool
herdlegsspeedgroup

Hop is to *rabbit* as

_____ is to *duck*.

runwaddleskiphopleapgallop
trotstridewhitewebbed

Poetry 21

A simile is a comparison that starts with *like* or *as*. Circle the simile.

The hill is grassy.

The grass is like a green blanket.

The grass is green.

The hill is high.

Poetry 22

Complete each simile.

The clouds are like _____

_____.

The grass is as _____

as _____.

The night sky is like _____

_____.

The thunder is like _____

_____.

Poetry 23

Write the missing words on the lines.

In a simile, you will always find the

word _____ or the

word _____.

Complete this sentence with a simile.

The baby lamb was _____

_____

_____.

Poetry

Poetry 24

The paper was as untouched as freshly fallen snow.

Name two ways a sheet of paper is like fresh snow.

_____

_____

_____

_____

Poetry 25

Write two sentences with similes.

_____

_____

_____

_____

_____

Poetry 26

In what way is a metaphor like a simile?

_____

_____

In what way is it different?

_____

_____

Poetry

Poetry 27

Put a check mark in front of the meaning of this sentence:

The cave is a refrigerator.

____ The cave is white and runs on electricity.

____ The cave is very cold.

____ The cave has a door with family photos on it.

Poetry 28

Circle the metaphor.

The children were as busy as ants at a picnic.

From the hilltop, the children looked like ants.

Far below on the playground, the children were ants.

Poetry 29

A simile or metaphor that people use all the time is called a *cliché*. It is usually better to use an original simile or metaphor. List four clichés.

_____

_____

_____

_____

_____

Poetry 30

Write a poem about your favorite number.

_____

_____

_____

_____

_____

_____

_____

Poetry

Poetry 31

Write two sentences with metaphors.

_____

_____

_____

_____

_____

Poetry 32

Write a poem about something that brings you good or bad luck.

_____

_____

_____

_____

_____

Poetry 33

Think of the multiplication fact that was hardest for you to learn. Write a poem about it.

_____

_____

_____

_____

_____

Poetry

Poetry 34

When poets use several words that begin with the same letter, the effect is called *alliteration*. List six words that begin with the letter *M*.

_____

_____

_____

_____

_____

_____

Poetry 35

Sometimes alliteration creates *onomatopoeia*, where the words make the sounds indicated when they are pronounced. Write a sentence that sounds like a snake hissing.

_____

_____

_____

_____

_____

_____

Poetry 36

Rewrite the sentence, changing the metaphor to a simile.

The rainbow is a bridge to the sky.

_____

_____

_____

_____

_____

Poetry 37

Rewrite the sentence, changing the simile to a metaphor.

The lake is like a mirror this morning.

_____

_____

_____

_____

_____

Poetry

Poetry 38

Hyperbole means exaggeration.
Circle the example of hyperbole in each sentence.

Jason is the meanest boy in the world.

My room was as cold as the South Pole.

Poetry 39

Write an example of hyperbole.

_____

_____

_____

_____

_____

_____

_____

_____

_____

Poetry 40

Circle the prepositional phrase in each sentence.

The deer bounded over the fence.

The car screeched around the corner.

The dog squeezed through a hole.

He hit the ball into centerfield.

Poetry 41

On your own paper, write a poem using this form:

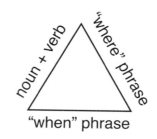

Poetry

Poetry 42

Accented and unaccented syllables create the rhythms of poetry. List three words with three syllables. Underline the stressed syllable in each word. For example: <u>syl</u> la ble

_____

_____

_____

Poetry 43

Poets create rhythm with repetition. On your own paper, write a poem with ten lines. The first nine lines will begin with the phrase "I hate ..." The last line will begin with "but I love ..."

Poetry 44

On your own paper, write a poem with nine lines that begin "With a million dollars I would buy ..." and a tenth line that begins "but even a million dollars can't buy ..."

Poetry 45

Write some sounds, smells, textures, and colors on the lines below, and then write a poem about a magic hallway on your own paper. Draw an illustration.

_____

_____

_____

_____

_____

_____

_____

Answer Keys

Building Blocks 1 (p.2)
Answers will vary.

Building Blocks 2 (p. 2)
friend - buddy
own - possess
couch - sofa
bird - fowl

Building Blocks 3 (p. 2)
is; was; were; are

Building Blocks 4 (p. 2)
beech - beach
prey - pray
inn - in
waste - waist

Building Blocks 5 (p. 3)
shriek; repeat; receive; limb; surprise

Building Blocks 6 (p. 3)
Answers will vary. Use something like: Sentences with action verbs are livelier, more interesting, and give more information.

Building Blocks 7–20 (p. 3–6)
Answers will vary.

Building Blocks 21 (p. 7)
except; all ready; desert; than

Building Blocks 22 (p. 7)
neice - niece; sinserly - sincerely; truely - truly; thout - thought; Febuary - February

Building Blocks 23 (p. 7)
possiblility; receive; bulletin; thieves

Building Blocks 24 (p. 7)
there; see; You're; know; Who's

Building Blocks 25–27 (p. 8)
Answers will vary.

Building Blocks 28 (p. 9)
I; Mr. Peters;
We; Grand Canyon; Uncle James;
Aunt Katie

Building Blocks 29 (p. 9)
Mrs. Hernandez reads to us every day after lunch. I missed the chapter yesterday because I had to see Dr. Lee. I sat next to Paulo at lunch. Stephen and Jamal sat with us too.

Building Blocks 30 (p. 9)
I like chocolate better than vanilla.

Everyday Writing 1 (p. 10)
heading (return address and date);
closing;
indent the paragraphs

Everyday Writing 2 (p. 10)
Yours Truely:
yours truly,
Sincerly Yours,

Everyday Writing 3 (p. 10)
302 Frog Ave.
Lupineville, CA 55555
April 24, 2020

Everyday Writing 4 (p. 10)
Answers will vary. Base scores on correct form.

Everyday Writing 5 (p. 11)
a. heading;
b. greeting;
c. body or text;
d. closing

Everyday Writing 6 (p. 11)
Answers will vary. Base score on correct form.

Everyday Writing 7 (p. 11)
a. return address;
b. inside address;
c. greeting;
d. body or text;
e. closing

Everyday Writing 8–11 (p. 12)
Answers will vary. Base score on correct form.

Everyday Writing 12 (p. 13)
Mr. William Arden
Middleville News
7650 Median St.
Middleville, AZ 50000
[Current month, date, year with no abbreviation]

Everyday Writing 13–16 (p. 13–14)
Answers will vary. Base score on correct form.

Everyday Writing 17 (p. 14)
due on April 24; 3–5 pages long;
use ink or word processor;
Subject: Education in the Colonies

Everyday Writing 18 (p. 14)
Friday, Oct. 5 at 7 p.m.; Talent Show!;
Eastgate School Auditorium;
$2 per person

Everyday Writing 19–30 (p. 14–17)
Answers will vary. Base score on correct form.

Everyday Writing 31 (p. 17)
exciting, suspense, battle, star, chase, fought

Everyday Writing 32–35 (p. 18)
Answers will vary. Base score on correct form.

Everyday Writing 36 (p. 19)
three reasons the war began

Everyday Writing 37 (p. 19)
how plants use light

Everyday Writing 38 (p. 19)
Questions will vary, but could include: What three kinds of tubes carry blood in the human body, and what is the special job of each?

Everyday Writing 39 (p. 20)
Answers will vary. Should have a topic sentence based on the question. *Example:* Every twenty-four hours, the earth turns on its axis. When our half of the earth faces the sun, it's day. When our half of the earth is turned away from the sun, it's night.

Everyday Writing 40–41 (p. 20)
Answers will vary but should have a topic sentence and at least one supporting sentence.

Everyday Writing 42 (p. 21)

There are thousands of kinds of insects. Insects have six legs. Their bodies are divided into three parts. An insect has a head, a thorax, and an abdomen. An ant is an insect, but a spider isn't.

Everyday Writing 43 (p. 21)

Water takes many forms. Water evaporates from the surface of the sea. It turns into clouds. Some of the water in clouds falls down as rain and snow. The rainwater runs downhill into rivers and streams until it reaches the sea. Water's journey is called the water cycle.

Everyday Writing 44–45 (p. 21)

Answers will vary but should have a topic sentence and at least one supporting sentence.

Nonfiction 1–11 (p. 22–25)

Answers will vary.

Nonfiction 12 (p. 25)

encyclopedia

Nonfiction 13 (p. 25)

Camels; the others are too broad or too narrow.

Nonfiction 14 (p. 25)

Answers will vary.

Nonfiction 15 (p. 26)

Causes of the Civil War; the others are too broad or too narrow.

Nonfiction 16 (p. 26)

encyclopedia or Internet to get an overview

Nonfiction 17 (p. 26)

information, author, page number, book title, publication date

Nonfiction 18 (p. 26)

It is acceptable to quote a sentence if you use quotation marks and give the source.

Nonfiction 19 (p. 27)

a personal interview, a pioneer diary, a soldier's letter

Nonfiction 20 (p. 27)

Use several sources because authorities don't always agree. Also, different sources include different kinds of supporting information.

Nonfiction 21 (p. 27)

Underline: solar system; eight planets; orbit, sun; Mercury, closest to sun; next, Venus, Earth, Mars; largest, Jupiter; Saturn, Uranus, Neptune, farthest away

Nonfiction 22 (p. 28)

I. Solar System
   A. Sun
   B. Planets
      1. Mercury
      2. Earth

Nonfiction 23–25 (p. 28)

Answers will vary.

Nonfiction 26 (p. 29)
Circle: [Native Americans gave a name to each full moon.]
Rewritten correctly: Native Americans gave a name to each full moon. January hosted the Wolf Moon. May basked under the Flower Moon. The Buck Moon graced July, and the Hunter's Moon illuminated October.

Nonfiction 27 (p. 29)
through; thorough; though

Nonfiction 28 (p. 29)
laid; lie; lay

Nonfiction 29 (p. 30)
lie; laid; lay

Nonfiction 30 (p. 20)
The parts of the ear are the outer ear, the eardrum, the cochlea, and the auditory nerve.

Nonfiction 31 (p. 30)
William Shakespeare died on April 23, 1616. He was fifty-two years old.

Nonfiction 32 (p. 31)
breath; breathe; except; accept

Nonfiction 33 (p. 31)
The legislative branch of our government makes laws.

Nonfiction 34 (p. 31)
There were fifty-five delegates to the Constitutional Convention, but many were absent.

Nonfiction 35 (p. 31)
In 1849, thousands of gold miners bought supplies and rushed to California.

Nonfiction 36 (p. 32)
Dolley Madison had to leave the White House because the British burned it down.

Nonfiction 37 (p. 32)
When immigrant Mormons couldn't afford covered wagons, they used handcarts.

Nonfiction 38 (p. 32)
George Washington, John Adams, and James Monroe were Presidents of the United States.

Nonfiction 39 (p. 33)
circles; is; drives; were

Nonfiction 40 (p. 33)
began; begin; crept; creeps; take; took

Fiction 1–28 (p. 34–41)
Answers will vary. Base score on appropriateness of answer and use of correct form.

Fiction 29 (p. 41)
the wicked stepmother/evil queen; Answers will vary.

Fiction 30–33 (p. 41–42)
Answers will vary. Base score on appropriateness of answer and use of correct form.

Fiction 34 (p. 42)
courage; kindness; loyalty; honesty; generosity

Fiction 35 (p. 43)
cheat, envy, hate, lazy, liar, lie (any four)

Fiction 36–40 (p. 43–44)
Answers will vary.

Poetry 1 (p. 45)
Answers will vary.

Poetry 2 (p. 45)
sand; sunflowers;
Answers will vary.

Poetry 3–6 (p. 45–46)
Answers will vary.

Poetry 7 (p. 46)
Sue; cow; zoo.
Limericks will vary.

Poetry 8 (p. 47)
Answers will vary.

Poetry 9 (p. 47)
wooly; glossy; slick; rough; leathery

Poetry 10 (p. 47)
quack, oink, woof, meow, squeak, honk, hum, neigh

Poetry 11 (p. 47)
emerald - green; scarlet - red; amber - yellow; sapphire - blue; amethyst - purple

Poetry 12 (p. 48)
Answers will vary.

Poetry 13 (p. 48)
An old cold.
Original hink pinks will vary.

Poetry 14–15 (p. 48)
Answers will vary.

Poetry 16 (p. 49)
fly; fan; can

Poetry 17 (p. 49)
quiet; to stop noise; unmoving; without waves; a photograph; continuing

Poetry 18 (p. 49)
thermometer; silverware

Poetry 19 (p. 49)
light; boy; short; day

Poetry 20 (p. 50)
pride; waddle

Poetry 21 (p. 50)
The grass is like a green blanket

Poetry 22 (p. 50)
Answers will vary.

Poetry 23 (p. 50)
like; as;
Similes will vary.

Poetry 24–25 (p. 51)
Answers will vary.

Poetry 26 (p. 51)
They both compare unlike things. A simile uses the word *like* or *as*; a metaphor doesn't.

Poetry 27 (p. 52)
The cave is very cold.

Poetry 28 (p. 52)
Far below on the playground, the
children were ants.

Poetry 29–35 (p. 52–54)
Answers will vary.

Poetry 36 (p. 54)
The rainbow is like a bridge to the sky.

Poetry 37 (p. 54)
The lake is a mirror this morning.

Poetry 38 (p. 55)
meanest boy in the world;
as cold as the South Pole

Poetry 39 (p. 55)
Answers will vary.

Poetry 40 (p. 55)
over the fence;
around the corner;
through a hole;
into centerfield

Poetry 41–45 (p. 55–56)
Answers will vary.